The Wild Horse Gatherers

written and photographed by Alden Robertson

Sierra Club Books/Charles Scribner's Sons   **San Francisco/New York**

The Wild Horse Gatherers was edited and prepared for publication at The Yolla Bolly Press, Covelo, California, under the supervision of James and Carolyn Robertson during the fall and winter months of 1977. Production staff: Gene Floyd, Jay Stewart, Loren Fisher, Joyca Cunnan, Diana Fairbanks.

The Sierra Club, founded in 1892 by John Muir, has devoted itself to the study and protection of the nation's scenic and ecological resources — mountains, woodlands, wild shores and rivers. All Club publications are part of the nonprofit effort the Club carries on as a public trust. There are some 50 chapters coast to coast, in Canada, Hawaii and Alaska. Participation is invited in the Club's program to enjoy and preserve wilderness everywhere. Address: 530 Bush Street, San Francisco, California 94108.

Manufactured in the United States of America

1 3 5 7 9 11 13 15 17 19 MD/C 20 18 16 14 12 10 8 6 4 2
1 3 5 7 9 11 13 15 17 19 MD/P 20 18 16 14 12 10 8 6 4 2

Library of Congress Cataloging in Publication Data

Robertson, Alden.
The wild horse gatherers.

SUMMARY: Text and photographs describe efforts of a small band of cowboys to round up wild horses and burros to prevent their growing numbers from overgrazing fragile desert land.

1. Wild horses — The West — Juvenile literature. 2. Donkeys — The West — Juvenile literature. 3. Cowboys — The West — Juvenile literature. 4. Wildlife conservation — The West — Juvenile literature. [1. Wild horses. 2. Donkeys. 3. Cowboys. 4. Wildlife conservation.]

I. Title.
SF284.U5R63   639'.97'9725   77-17512
ISBN 0-684-15589-3
ISBN 0-684-15591-5 pbk.

**To Breon,
who is both my son
and best friend.**

About Wild Horses

The land has a coarse, wasted look, as does much of the country just east of the Sierra Nevada. The soil is mostly sand and rock, and the vegetation is sparse. It has not rained much out here, so the bright green of new grass is missing. Just the same, it is awe-inspiring country with grand vistas, however bleak and formidable they might appear.

I was standing on a Nevada mountainside above my riding partner, Merv Coleman, looking east toward the Smoke Creek Desert and the mountains of the Fox Range beyond. Out on the flat, about two miles away and below us, was a cowboy, Vern Carson. He was chasing wild horses. He was trying to work a small group of about seven of them up to where we were waiting on the eastern slope of Twin Peaks.

For a while we had been able to follow his progress by watching the dust kicked up by the horses as they ran. Now no longer able to see anything, we could only listen to Vern talking over the radio to another cowboy, his boss Gene Nunn, who was on the ridge behind us. Gene had binoculars and was trying to help Vern by spotting for him. Much of the time Vern could not even see the horses he was after, so Gene would try to tell him where they were and the direction they were headed in. It felt strange to be standing on that cold, quiet mountain, seeing no sign of life but hearing Vern's voice, out of breath, giving a running account of the chase going on out there somewhere.

To catch the horses, we had to run them into a trap, or corral, located behind us on the opposite side of the mountain. But before we could do that, Vern had to get them up to Gene. Then Gene would take over and keep the horses moving toward the trap where a third

7

Vern is a tough, leathery little fifty-year-old ex-cab driver from Baltimore, Maryland. Years ago he began learning about horses while working around Maryland racetracks. He enjoys what he does for a living now. Vern says he would rather run wild horses than do anything else in the world.

I do not think I can adequately describe Willard Jones, but I will try. Willard can seldom be caught with a straight face. That is to say, his disposition is generally happy and causes him to smile and laugh a lot. He is also never at a loss for words. This particular photo of Willard is quite rare since he is neither smiling, laughing, or talking. Maybe it was just too early in the morning for any of that.

cowboy was waiting to follow them on in and close the gate. The total distance traveled would be over five miles. It seemed to me like a very ambitious plan.

As expected, the horses finally started moving up the slope in our direction, following a route which had also been anticipated. The cowboys know that wild horses nearly always run to high ground when pursued and prefer to travel on already established trails. Suddenly we saw the horses off on our left, to the north, moving along a trail which would bring them above and behind us, just as planned. They were moving fast now and had left Vern far behind. We watched the horses disappear into a ravine just above us. When they reappeared they veered in our direction.

We rode toward them shouting and waving our arms, hoping they would shy away uphill, toward Gene. Instead they broke into a full gallop and came straight at us. It was every horse for himself and may the devil take the hindmost as they scattered and went flying by us on all sides. It was as if we weren't even there. In an instant all the horses were clear of us and already regrouping on the other side. As they ran off into the distance, I thought I could see a little high stepping here and there and a tail or two held out at a smart angle.

I expected the radio to explode with curses, especially from Vern who had worked so hard to get the horses up the mountain. Instead he simply turned around and rode back down to start all over again. The rest of us settled down to wait. If it was our fault that we couldn't turn the horses, the cowboys didn't rub it in by telling us about it. It seemed possible though that not even the cowboys could have kept those horses from making their escape.

12

Gene Nunn came from Montana to help start the wild horse and burro program in Susanville. He had been doing the same kind of work on the BLM's Pryor Mountain Wild Horse Range, located on the border of Montana and Wyoming. You might spend days with Gene and the cowboys before realizing that he was their boss. When a decision needs to be made, it is done quickly and quietly. The rest of the time everyone seems to know what needs doing, and they simply do it.

Wild horses are feral animals, which means they are domestic animals gone wild, or domestic animals whose ancestors, at one time or another, became wild. The Spaniards are credited with bringing the first horses to this continent. Their horses were small, tough little animals, originally from nothern Africa, called Barbary horses or Barbs. Certain Native American tribes were able to acquire some of these horses, and by the time the pioneers began moving west, the Plains Indians had for some time been carried on their nomadic travels by descendants of these Barbary horses. The pioneers, settlers, and soldiers all brought horses to the West and, as had the Spaniards and Indians before them, they all lost horses which subsequently became wild.

The Spanish use the term *mestengo* to describe a stray animal, such as one of their Barbs, which had escaped from its owner. English-speaking settlers evidently could not pronounce that word but tried and it came out "mustang." We still call the wild horses mustangs, but there is little chance that more than a trace of the Barbary horse lingers in the bloodlines of the wild horses found today. Horses are still running away, from ranchers for instance, and they need little encouragement to revert to a wild state. Ask anyone who has chased a saddle horse around a pasture, halter in one hand and a bucket of oats in the other. So the horses we were chasing on Twin Peaks that day were wild horses whose history could surely be traced to a period of domestication, perhaps so recent that one or another might be wearing the brand of a local rancher. But where they came from seemed unimportant as we watched the horses running wild across that Nevada mountainside. There is little for us to see these days that can stir the imagination quite as much.

Bob Budesa is the youngest of the cowboys. Gene hopes that he will still be around when some of the other, older cowboys have retired. He is also the only one with a college degree. That doesn't keep the others from giving him a bit of advice now and then, and it doesn't keep him from listening either.

People have been chasing wild horses in Nevada and other parts of the western United States for as long as there have been wild horses to chase. When the horse was still an important and necessary part of our lives, there was an obvious reason for this, and captured horses were put to good use. In recent years however, wild horses have been less sought for use as domestic animals than as a source of food for pets. This disturbed enough people that together they were able to persuade Congress to pass legislation protecting wild horses and also the wild burros who share the range with the horses. In 1971 this legislation became law. It was called the Wild Free-Roaming Horse and Burro Act. The Forest Service and the Bureau of Land Management were made responsible for the wild horses and burros on public land.

The Bureau of Land Management (BLM) is a federal agency, a branch of the Department of the Interior. As its name implies, it manages public land. One of its major functions is to maintain a balance between the number of animals, both wild and domestic, grazing on public land and the ability of the grazing land to support these animals. According to the BLM, the fact that wild horses and burros are now protected has caused a rapid increase in their numbers. Overgrazing has reportedly resulted, which now poses a threat to the well-being of the horses, the animals with which they share the range, and the range itself. In order to improve the balance, the BLM has decided that the wild horse and burro herds must be thinned in some areas. The animals are captured, removed from the range, and offered for adoption. It is the job of Gene, Vern, and the rest of the cowboys who work for the BLM to gather the wild horses. I was there to photograph them and write about their work.

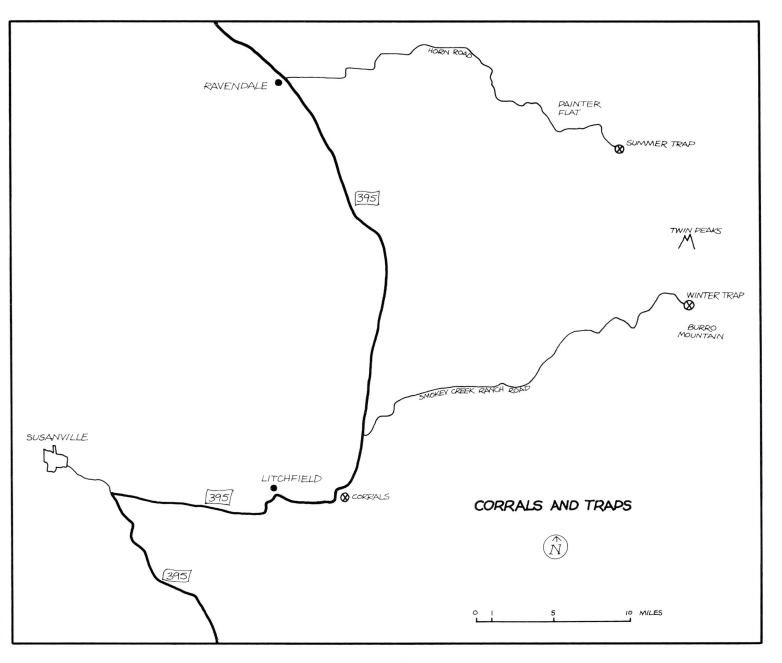

RAVENDALE

HORN ROAD

PAINTER
FLAT

⊗ SUMMER TRAP

395

TWIN PEAKS
M

WINTER TRAP ⊗

BURRO
MOUNTAIN

SMOKEY CREEK RANCH ROAD

SUSANVILLE

LITCHFIELD

395

⊗ CORRALS

CORRALS AND TRAPS

Ⓝ

0   1   5   10   MILES

It had snowed the day before, but there was bare ground showing through the patches of white, making it hard to tell the horses from the background. The cowboys are always looking for horses on the drive from the corrals out to the trap and can generally spot them with no trouble at all, while I squint into the distance, unable to see a thing unless it happens to be running around in circles at the time. On this particular morning, even the cowboys were having trouble making anything out.

Sunrise Every Morning

I made two trips to Susanville, in northeastern California, to visit the cowboys. The first was in early March. I met them at the BLM office in Susanville early one morning. It was 5:30, cold and dark. They meet there every morning at that hour to pick up the trucks they will use during the day. The trucks are used for their own transportation and also to haul horses. The cowboys always need at least two trucks and sometimes as many as three or more. We drove east out of town to some corrals near Litchfield on Highway 395. The sun was just coming up when we arrived. The cowboys get to see the sunrise every morning.

The corrals are where the recently captured wild horses and burros are kept, as well as the cowboys' saddle horses. It is part of the cowboys' job to take care of all these animals, so the first thing they did that morning was to feed them and make sure they had water. Then they ran the saddle horses into a pen and caught and haltered the ones they wanted to ride that day. The horses don't exactly volunteer for duty, so trying to get close enough to put a halter on one of them can get a little exciting. It looked to me like a real good way to get run over or kicked in the head, but it didn't seem to bother the cowboys. Once haltered, the horses were led back to the tack room where they were brushed and saddled. It was not yet eight o'clock when they loaded the horses into the trailer and left for the trap.

The trap was located just below Burro Mountain Pass, between Twin Peaks and Burro Mountain. We were still gathering on Twin Peaks, but after losing that bunch of horses on the eastern side of the mountain, we moved over to the western side. Gene thought the horses on the eastern slopes of Twin Peaks would probably stay there despite our best efforts to catch them. They were getting too smart, and the more we chased them, the smarter they would get. The horses on the other side were probably just as smart, but one morning we got lucky.

Willard and I were just pulling up to the trap behind Bob and Vern when they suddenly began backing up, frantically motioning for us to stop. They came tiptoeing back to our truck, all bent over as if trying to make themselves invisible. In whispers they explained that they had just seen some horses standing practically in the trap. We were parked with a hill between us and the horses, so if the cowboys were real sneaky they could probably get very close to the horses before being seen. They unloaded their own horses as quietly as possible, tightened the cinches on their saddles, and rode off. I stayed by the trap and waited.

Before long I saw the wild horses running along the ridge. They had been much lower down on the slope, but the minute they saw the cowboys they headed straight uphill. They paused at the top, looking toward the wing fence, and finally turned and followed it down the hill and right into the corral. At that moment Bob and Willard came galloping up and closed the gate behind them. It was all so quick and simple that I felt a little cheated.

The terrain itself is used to help funnel the horses into the trap, but light, rope-wing fences are also used. The trap itself is open at one end and closed at the other, with a loading ramp at the closed end. It is really a long series of pens with gates in between. The first group of horses will be run all the way to the far end of the trap and a gate closed behind this group. Then the next group will be run into the trap as far as the first gate, and another gate closed behind it, and so on until all the pens are full. At that point the gathering will stop for the day, and the horses will be loaded into trucks and hauled back to the corrals at Litchfield.

But if it was easy that once, it seemed just the opposite all the other times we went out gathering that week. We spent long hours on horseback, not only just walking along but when the chase was at close quarters, galloping through brush and over loose, jagged rocks the size of footballs. That sort of riding was very hard on the horses, and if one got too tired or lamed up, its rider walked. Often a cowboy had to switch to his spare horse partway through the day, and sometimes he wore that one out as well. The other cowboys, those who waited for the wild horses somewhere along their expected route, just sat around in the cold. They always kept matches with them and built a fire if they had to, but there was nothing they could do about the waiting.

One day we had all been waiting for Willard to chase some horses in our direction, but all the horses he got moving, headed the wrong way. We were all talking to one another over our radios, but the only sign I could see of anyone else was a little wisp of smoke from the fire Vern had built to keep from freezing. I was riding around trying to keep warm and, with binoculars, spotted two large groups of horses about two miles away. Just then Willard began talking excitedly over the radio about all the horses he was seeing. As I watched, both of the groups I had spotted suddenly broke into a gallop. Willard shouted, "If we don't catch this bunch, we'll sure as hell scatter them all over the place."

I never did spot Willard, but he was obviously after the horses I was watching — and scatter them we did. By the time the cowboys got up to where we were waiting, there were horses all over the place and not much anyone could do to keep them going toward the trap. In all the confusion, Vern did get close enough to

rope a horse, but that one and another he roped later on in the day were the only horses we caught. Some days we didn't catch any.

When horses were caught, they were loaded into trucks and driven back to the corrals at Litchfield. That was always a long, slow trip because most of it was on dirt roads. By the time the wild horses were unloaded and penned and the saddle horses unloaded, unsaddled, checked and, if necessary, doctored for cuts, it was often six or seven in the evening and sometimes later. Gene used to say that the cowboys were told it was going to be an eight to five job when they hired on, so he couldn't understand the complaints just because they were working from five to eight instead. Of course there were no complaints. Vern seemed to be speaking for all the cowboys, Gene included, when he told me he would rather run horses than do anything else.

I think I was beginning to understand why. When the cowboys arrive at the trap, step out of the trucks, and climb onto their horses to ride out in search of wild horses, they have ridden into another time, leaving behind almost all traces of the twentieth century. There is nothing out there to remind them that at the other end of the long dirt road that brought them there, Highway 395 is waiting to take them back to Susanville or on to Reno or Los Angeles or wherever it is that the rest of us live and work. Their sojourn into the Nevada desert, however short, is something all of us can envy.

A Change in the Game

On that first trip we spent three days gathering horses and caught just ten. Most of that time there were only three cowboys working instead of the usual four or five, so we might have done better with a full crew of riders. But at best, the average catch is only three or four horses per day. The problem is that wild horses are too fast and have too much room in which to make their escape.

When I returned to Susanville the following July, the situation had changed and the wild horses no longer enjoyed the advantage of their speed or the freedom provided by an almost boundless country. The BLM team was pursuing them with a helicopter.

Some of the cowboys, when put on the spot, admitted that they would rather be out there on their own without the helicopter. I think the work must have been more satisfying that way — the old way. On the other hand, I didn't hear any of them say they couldn't use the help. They were certainly catching more horses with the helicopter than they had without, which is why the BLM had decided to use it.

So now Gene rides in a helicopter giving directions to the pilot, while the rest of the cowboys, still on horseback, wait for him to bring the horses to them at the trap. And bring them he does, as many as forty or more horses in one day.

The trap had been moved to an area called Painter Flat. To get there from the corrals at Litchfield, we drove north on Highway 395 for an hour to Ravendale, a little place consisting of a motel; a combination cafe, bar, gas station; and a few houses. It is the home base and watering place for the cowboys when they are working in the area. From Ravendale we turned east and bounced along a dirt road for another hour before arriving at the trap. By the time we arrived, it was eight in the morning, and the sun was high enough to begin warming things up.

Shortly after we got there, Gene went off in the helicopter. Before long he reappeared with a small bunch of horses. The new trap was situated in such a way that one wing fence closed off the end of a shallow little valley between two low-lying hills. Willard waited back down the valley, away from the trap and out of sight. As the helicopter moved the horses past him, he fell in behind and kept them going toward the trap. B.T. Frost, a recent addition to the group, and Bob Budesa each covered one of the two wing fences. When the horses got to the trap, B.T. and Bob joined Willard and followed them on in to close the gate.

This procedure was repeated twice more before we stopped for lunch. The work was going quickly because Gene had been able to find horses within a half mile of the trap. Not only that, but they were cooperative and easily moved. So far we had captured twenty-six horses.

Gene went out again right after lunch but this time was gone for much longer than before. Finally he came back with just four horses, three mares and a big, shiny black stud that looked like Black Beauty. They had given Gene and the pilot fits, refusing to be hurried and always trying to turn back or uphill, never

30

Each of the three groups we gathered that morning was composed of a single stud, his mares, and their foals. This family group will range from six to ten horses and is the most predominant grouping we found. There are also bachelor groups of young studs, about the same size as the family groups, but they are not as common.

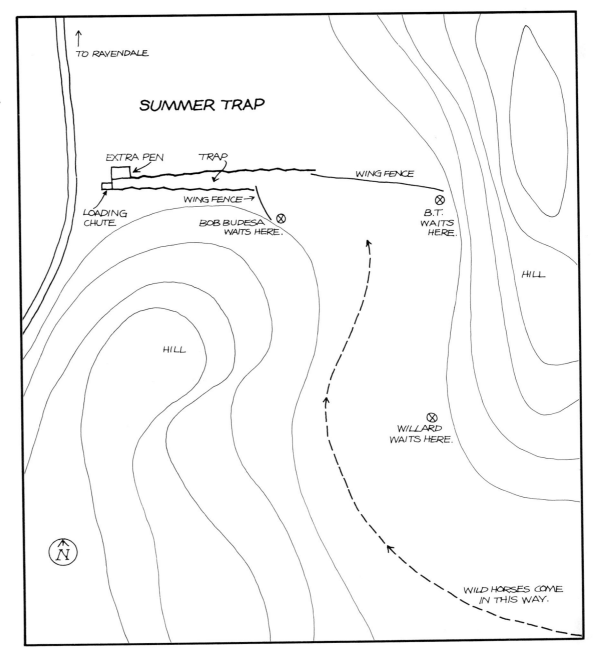

SUMMER TRAP

B.T. Frost grew up in southeast Colorado. His father used to travel around the countryside in a wagon buying and trading horses. On the weekends, B.T. would herd the horses his father had acquired back to their home. His afternoons after school were spent breaking these horses for his father. B.T. left ranch work for a while before he came to Susanville. He needed the money so he took a job in an oil field. He was earning almost twice as much as he does now but he hated the work. He says that he was so unhappy he began to drink a great deal. When he realized what he was doing to himself, he quit and went back to doing what he liked most—being a cowboy.

traveling in a straight line. They were eventually run into the trap and the gate closed behind them, but a few minutes later the three mares suddenly decided to have a go at the fence.

The cowboys were just outside the gate talking about how much trouble this piddling little group of horses had been, speaking in the past tense as though it was all over. I was sitting on top of the fence, facing outside, about thirty feet from where the mares were standing, bunched up right against the same fence. All of a sudden I heard snorting and stamping and felt the fence start to tip under me! As I jumped off, I looked over and saw the mares half jumping and half climbing over the fence. They didn't even bother to take a run at it but instead tried a sort of standing high jump. With their hooves clanging loudly against the pipe rails of the fence, they pushed it partway over and disappeared almost instantly into the brush.

The fence remained enough of a barrier to keep the stud from escaping as well — I think he must have been as surprised as the rest of us. All we could do was shout and curse but there wasn't even time for much of that. And we couldn't do much about retrieving the mares, either. In any case, they had already taken more expensive helicopter time than their capture was worth.

I will have to admit it pleased me to discover that the horses could still occasionally win at this game. But I was sorry Black Beauty could not have joined his mares.

Gene decided that we should quit before we had any more bad luck. He was not very happy with a catch of just twenty-seven horses which probably barely justified the use of the helicopter. He was also a little angry with himself for not dropping the black stud and his

39

three mares and going on to find another group, when he realized how difficult those four were going to be to move. I think the right decision was more obvious looking back on it than it had been earlier when he was up in the helicopter. After loading the horses into a truck and seeing them off to the corrals, we drove into Ravendale where we would spend the night.

On the following day the gathering got off to a slow start. Actually it was a horrible start. The first bunch of horses Gene brought in were spooked by something as they ran up to the fence on the right side of the trap. Whatever they saw was off to the left and kept them from going in that direction into the trap. Instead they went straight ahead, right over the fence, knocking down about 150 feet of it! B.T. was galloping along parallel to the fence and rode right up to the horses as they reached it. Just as he got there, they all disappeared in a thick cloud of dust making it impossible for B.T. to see the horse he was riding, let alone the wild horses a few feet away. When he rode out the other side, he was sure they had vanished into thin air. It took him a moment to notice the fence was down and the horses were running pell-mell down the valley toward Painter Flat. We were an hour or more setting the fence back up, and by the time Gene climbed into the helicopter for another try, it was late.

By noon, two small groups totaling seventeen horses were run in, and then Gene decided to go farther afield and work in a new area. Within forty-five minutes he brought in two groups of horses, but this time there were more of them, thirty-two in all. And with that sudden change in luck — forty-nine horses captured in one day — we finished gathering with enough animals to keep the cowboys busy at the corrals for the rest of the week.

This is the corral at Ravendale where the cowboys
keep their saddle horses
when staying overnight.

Gene, on the left, may not look like much of a pool player but he is. In fact he could probably make a little money at it, in Ravendale at least. He and I were partners in this game, and even though I didn't help much, we won.

It is still dark when the cowboys eat breakfast in Ravendale. Bob, on the left, is listening to Gene, Willard, and B.T. discuss their chances of catching lots of horses on that day, their last day at the trap that week.

One morning in Ravendale the cowboys went to the corral to get their horses— and they were gone! They had gotten into a large pasture in the rear. The horses ran around for ten or fifteen minutes and had a great time. Willard and B.T. didn't seem to enjoy it nearly as much.

All that remained was to load those horses into trucks for the trip back to Litchfield. Loading turned out to be no easy job. Trying to coax a bunch of wild and fearful animals into strange-looking contraptions like the trucks requires considerable yelling, prodding, and waving of arms. Clouds of dust swirled around the men and horses, adding to the confusion. There seems to be no other way to accomplish the task, however, and the cowboys work with the skill of much experience. For the horses, it is a rude introduction to the domestic way of life which they have for so long, and perhaps with good reason, avoided.

At the Corrals

After spending the first two days of the week gathering at the trap, the cowboys spent the following three days at the corrals working with the horses they had just captured.

When the horses are brought to the corrals from the trap, they are put in small holding pens. The studs are generally penned up with their mares and, whenever possible, kept apart from one another. If two studs do happen to end up in the same pen and start knocking one another around, they will be separated.

The mares are never separated from their foals unless by accident. If that happens, the cowboys are always able to remember which mare is the foal's mother. It is a wonder to me that they can do this because when I look at the horses all I see are a bunch of wild animals, all of which look pretty much the same. But the cowboys see much more than I do. They see individual horses, each with different characteristics of age, color, conformation, and temperament. And because of this, they are apt to recognize a foal and remember having seen it with a particular mare. In any case, the horses are not kept long in separate pens and are soon turned out to pasture.

Early Wednesday at the corrals, after the morning chores were done and their horses saddled and ready to go, the cowboys began the real work of the day. Before starting on the new horses, there were a couple of other things that had to be taken care of. First they ran all the horses from one of the pastures into the main corral and separated out a few horses that had been chosen for adoption and some others requiring blood tests. The adopted horses were put in a pen by themselves and would remain there until their new owners picked them up. The other horses were going to be sent to Chincoteague, Virginia, where they will be used to strengthen the breed of small wild horses which already lives on the island. The cowboys had only to rope these horses so that a vet could take a blood sample to test for equine infectious anemia. Most states require this test before allowing any horse entrance. One by one the Chincoteague horses were "headed and heeled," that is, roped around the neck and hind legs and dropped to the ground where a blood sample was taken. It was all done quickly and the vet's assistants were busy keeping records and running syringes back and forth. Then we started the more involved process of branding the new horses waiting in the holding pens.

First the cowboys opened the gate and let them out of the pens — either one at a time or a mare and her

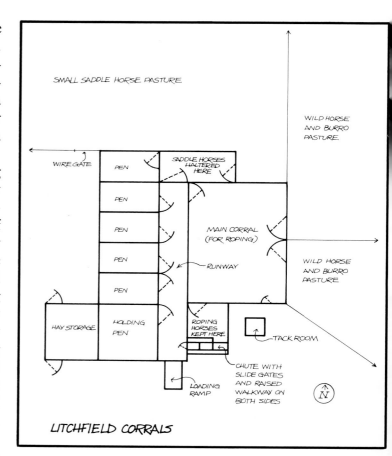

LITCHFIELD CORRALS

Gene is in the runway
which connects all the
holding pens to the main
corral. He is looking for
horses whose numbers are
on the list he is holding.
The list, made up at the
Susanville office of the
BLM, is of applications re-
ceived from people who
want to adopt horses.

The cowboys will trade jobs a number of times during the day. The roping is done by two cowboys at a time, and two others work on the ground doing the marking. When their saddle horses begin to tire, the cowboys who are roping will give them a rest and work as the ground crew, while the other two cowboys take their turn roping. Generally Gene and B.T. worked as one team and Bob and Willard the other. It was a favorite trick of both teams to quit roping and start walking when the next horse to be dealt with was a great big mean-looking stud.

A young horse that Bob
was trying to rope went
through the fence here.
The horse didn't even hesi-
tate; it just ran up to the
fence full tilt, jumped
right through it, and kept
going into the pasture on
the other side without so
much as a stumble. It
scared the heck out of Bob.
He was afraid the horse
was going to kill itself.

foal together — and into the corral. There each was roped and dropped to the ground where it could be worked on. Among the first few horses out was a mare and her foal, a big stout colt. Gene and B.T. were roping, B.T. taking the head and Gene coming along to catch the hind legs. B.T. got the mare running along one side of the corral right up against the fence, made a good throw at her head, and caught her. The colt had been running at her side, but when the mare started jumping around at the end of B.T.'s rope, he decided to get the heck out of there and moved to the other side of the corral. B.T. had to keep the mare moving so that Gene could catch the hind legs. The way he did it was to throw a big loop across in front of the legs, actually right up against them, and when the horse stepped into it, he jerked the slack out of the rope so that the loop tightened around the legs. But Gene was having a bad day and had to take a number of shots at the mare before he finally succeeded in heeling her. I don't think it helped much to have the ground crew, Willard and Bob, hooting and hollering and loudly counting each time he missed a throw.

As soon as Gene and B.T. brought the mare down, it was time for Bob and Willard to go to work. Their job was to brand her and determine her age. This information, along with the sex, color, and any distinctive markings, was recorded for every wild horse brought into the corrals. A horse's age is determined by an examination of the teeth. Of course you have to know what to look for. It has something to do with whether or not a horse still has baby teeth, and if so, which ones. A horse will lose different baby teeth at certain times, but when all those teeth are gone and the permanent teeth are in, it becomes a real guessing game. Then what you do is look at the cups in the

One or maybe both of these ropes were intended for the horse's head and ended up at the hind legs. They will soon be kicked off, and the cowboys will start all over again. The fellow in the cap is a local rancher who comes around whenever he can to help the cowboys rope.

B.T. got the rope jerked out of his hand after heeling a horse, and by the time the horse kicked it off, the loop had come undone. He is stringing another loop here. All the cowboys are choosey about the rope they use. Some like a stiffer rope than others. Some like a rope that is longer than others, and so on. But I never heard even one of the cowboys try to excuse a missed throw by blaming it on his rope.

Once a horse is down, the rope around its neck is removed and put around the front legs, making it impossible for the animal to get up while the cowboys are working on it.

Willard, hidden behind the foal he is wrestling, has his work cut out for him. He is trying to drop the colt to the ground so that Bob can prepare it for freeze marking.

teeth. These cups are in the top or grinding surface of the teeth, and as a horse gets older and its teeth wear down, the cups become more shallow.

I guess the cowboys have looked in lots of horses' mouths because most of them are very quick at telling a horse's age. But that morning some cowboy from out of town who had been around all week trying to help was in the corral with Bob and Willard and had taken the job of determining the age of each horse. He was down on his knees, bending over the mare's head, and was fishing around in her mouth with his finger, trying to dig the dirt out of the cups in her teeth. Suddenly he straightened up, gave a yell, and started hopping up and down in the middle of the corral, cursing and shouting. Willard, who had been down on the ground next to him, looked over his shoulder at us and calmly announced that the mare had just bitten off the end of the guy's finger. Nobody blamed the mare for what she had done, and after the dust settled, I think the victim was thankful she hadn't taken a bigger bite.

When everyone had recovered from that excitement, Bob and Willard got on with the branding. The brand is a simple C-2, designating California, District Number Two, the BLM district in which the mare was caught. The mark itself, placed high on the right-hand side of the neck, is not the usual hot brand but a freeze mark. For this kind of brand the marking iron is cooled to below freezing in liquid nitrogen. The freeze mark changes the pigmentation of the hair rather than leaving a scar on the hide as does a hot iron.

To make exact identification possible, the mare was also marked with a numbered paper tag which was glued to her rump. This number stays on each horse for as long as it remains at the BLM corrals and is

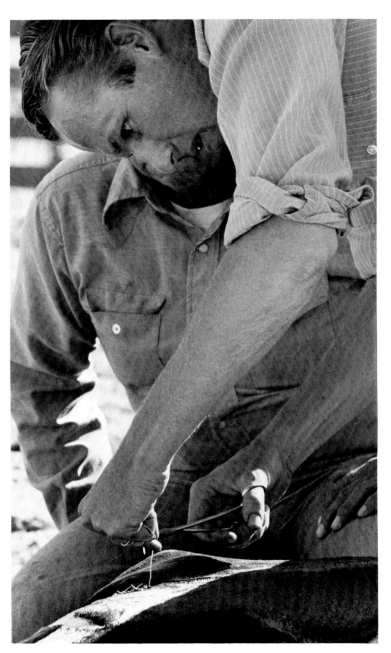

This mare evidently brushed up against a nail head in the fence and laid open a big triangular shaped patch on her shoulder. Dr. Pyle explained that horses, compared to cattle, are very thin skinned. His young assistants look a little squeamish here, and good old B.T. seems about to faint.

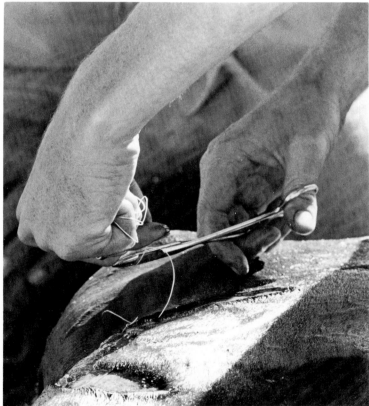

recorded along with its description. When a horse with particular characteristics is requested for adoption, the people at the BLM simply go through the records to find a similar animal. The cowboys will then be provided with that horse's description and number, enabling them to locate it easily.

When the recording and marking were finished, B.T. and Gene gave the mare some slack in her ropes so that she could get to her feet. The rope around her neck had been moved earlier to her front legs, and as soon as she was standing, she stepped out of both loops and ran out of the corral. She went through the gate Bob had opened for her and into the pasture on the other side, nickering softly and somewhat reassuringly to her foal. It was his turn next. He was roped around his neck and then Willard proceeded to wrestle him to the ground. As large and sturdy as he was, they could have heeled him as they did his mother, but it is easier on a young animal and sometimes quicker if a man on the ground throws it down by hand. In this case it wasn't quicker, and while it might have been easier on the colt, it was real rough on Willard. He said this one made him see stars. Bob then trimmed a spot on the colt's neck with hair clippers, swabbed the spot with alcohol, and Willard marked it there with the freeze iron.

After a number was glued onto the colt's rear end, he was run into the pasture to join his mother, who was waiting for him at the gate. They will remain there in relative peace and properly cared for, until the day someone arrives to take them to a new home and a different life. And the cowboys will return to Painter Flat or Fox Hog Mountain or High Rock or some other place in that wide-open country where there are still wild horses to gather.

These high school kids are spending their summer working for the Youth Conservation Corps. They spent the morning at the BLM office in Susanville watching a slide show about the wild horse program and are now seeing a bit of it firsthand. They will also get to build a whole bunch of fence for Gene, who is here answering questions for them.

Gene and B.T. moved some of the Chincoteague horses to an old ranch southeast of the corrals where they remained until all forty were ready to ship. It was very quiet and peaceful, and the horses seemed content there.

Although it is now run
down and slowly falling
apart, the High Rock Ranch
must have once been a very
fine place. There is still
enough left here to inspire
anyone to dream about
owning a place as nice.

I wonder though if there will always be wild horses to gather and cowboys to do the gathering. Our world is changing so fast that someday there may not be a place in it for creatures such as wild horses and people such as cowboys. I hope there will be. They are too important for us to lose. Both the horses and the men who tend them are reminders that no matter how far away the modern age may take us from cowboys and their work, we are still earth's creatures and, like the wild horses, still depend on what the earth provides to maintain our lives.

Acknowledgments

I hope the cowboys realize how much I appreciate their patience, humor, and friendship. Considering how often they must put up with journalists and photographers, it is a wonder to me that they were still willing to have anything to do with this tenderfoot. Without their cooperation, doing this book would have been difficult, if not impossible. I thank them all: Gene Nunn, Willard Jones, B.T. Frost, Bob Budesa, and Vern Carson.

I would also like to thank Connie Kingston and the rest of the people in the Susanville office of the BLM who were so helpful.

Author's Note

At the time this book was printed, the Bureau of Land Management was offering horses for adoption to any person who can meet certain qualifications. For those of you who may be interested in adopting a horse, I have a bit of advice to offer. It is no easy thing to gentle and train a wild horse — or any horse for that matter. It requires a huge amount of determination and more patience than most of us possess. But, as with any hard task, the rewards are also great, if you do the job well. For more information regarding the Adopt-A-Horse Program, write: Adopt-A-Horse, Bureau of Land Management, Denver Service Center, Denver Federal Center, Building 50, Denver, Colorado 80225.

Afterword

About forty million years ago, *Eohippus,* the first ancestor of the horse, evolved on the Great Plains in North America. This shy creature was about the size of a cat and had four toes, instead of hooves, on each foot. Over millions of years it grew and developed until it reached the size of a small horse today. Then during the Ice Ages, horses and other animals migrated to Asia — and from there to other parts of the world. By 6000 B.C. the horse was extinct in the Western Hemisphere.

The Spanish conquistadores first brought horses back to North America in 1519, and the settlers who later crossed the Plains from the East brought many more. Over the centuries some escaped and became wild. The cowboys we meet in this book are rounding up the distant descendants of these horses.

You might ask, as many people do: Why not leave these wild horses as they are, running free? Those who support the rounding up of the wild horses answer that the horses are multiplying faster than the lands they roam on can grow grass to feed them. This causes overgrazing, which leads in turn to erosion of the soil and overcrowding of the horses. Another problem, they say, is that too great a number of horses, and burros too, compete for food and water with native species (animals that lived in the region before the horses came back to it) such as the pronghorn antelope. This could endanger these creatures' chances for survival.

It is not easy to tell just how many wild horses there are, and the people who would like to leave the horses alone often disagree about this with those who would like to see the herds reduced. That is one of the difficulties we face in solving the problem. On the other hand, most people agree about the need to protect the land and its native creatures while treating the horses humanely at the same time. That is why many concerned people think the BLM's program of rounding the horses up and putting them out for adoption is a good one.

Even people who care deeply about wild lands and wild creatures cannot always find easy answers to such complicated questions as the effects of wild horses on the lands they inhabit. But they know that similar problems happen in many other places and situations. When men first come to a totally wild place, as the American pioneers came to the West, they rarely stop to think about the changes they set in motion in the natural balance, and sometimes years and years go by before anyone notices a problem. We might wish that the horses had not gotten loose in the first place, because then we wouldn't have this problem, but we probably wouldn't like it if there were no horses at all. Just wishing about the wild horses — or about saving whales, or getting rid of smog, or a thousand other problems — won't solve them. And when the first attempts are made to do something, they will hardly ever please everyone.

But when something *is* done, like the roundups and the Adopt-A-Horse Program, it makes more people know about what is happening, just as you do from reading this book. And among those people who get interested in the problem, there may be some who will finally help to solve it — to everyone's satisfaction.

Jon Beckmann
Sierra Club Books